Prophetic Order:
How Prophets and Pastors Can Work Together

Sharon Sarles

P.O. Box 971 Cedar Park, Texas 78630

Sarles, Sharon
Prophetic Order: How Prophets and Pastors Can Work Together
70 p. 23 cm.
1. Prophecy 2. Liturgy 3. Church Management 3. Etiquette – Church 4.
Mysticism – Christian 5. Evangelism - Practical
BV 652   254.

ISBN-13: 978-0965777018
ISBN-10 : 0-9657770-1-4

DEDICATION

To Bill and Wanda Rankin, great saints of God and good friends.

CONTENTS

PREFACE

Pastors, prophets, let us agree. We are commanded to seek the gifts. Praise God, finally, much of the Body of Christ has discovered this. However, there seems to be some confusion about how to operate in these manifestations of the Spirit. Rather than either retreating in fear or blundering forward in a wrong direction, please consider with me both Scripture and recent experience and consider some helpful ways forward.

The first thought to write this books was elicited by the disorder I have seen coming out of the "schools of the prophets" Indeed, I started, but the first manuscript was lost. I had also been importuned to offer mentoring in the prophetic, and only too late clearly saw that need and opportunity. My apologies. Then recently, I attended a conference where the hostess, a leading prophet and/or apostle, led a discussion about how prophets should interface with pastors. I was amazed that the lessons I thought well learned in the 1980s still were unknown to many. Lastly, I recently visited with the most trustworthy prophet I know, who is now elderly. I wanted to be sure I garnered her wisdom. I apprehend it is now time to write, in order to share and better spread good order, and feel I now have the timing of the Lord.

It is my intention to air problems only toward fixing them, not to lay down restraints so much as to show a health way forward.

Austin, Texas 2016

1 Seek Spiritual Gifts

It should be firmly established and kept in mind that we are commanded, **commanded of the Lord** mind you, to diligently seek after spiritual gifts (I Corinthians 12:1). Following the literal Greek, we should *lust* after the gifts. For the edifying of the Body of Christ.

It does not say "be open to the gifts." It clearly does say not to forbid speaking in tongues! It does not say that prophecy is a special gift that you may have if you are specially holy or especially ambitious. Certainly it does say that it is not for your own aggrandizement. Mark you this well. It is not for your own aggrandizement. You may indeed find gifts and use them so, but it will eventually mar them and endanger you if your character is not developed appropriately. Nevertheless, we are to seek to share these gifts. Prophecy is the gift most highly prized, because it is most clearly the one that communicates God's word to the people. Well, perhaps the most useful is the one most useful in the situation, but overall, prophecy tops the list of the 12.

Any good book on prophetic order will start with Paul's words in Corinthians, but first let us define our terms. Many people wish to dismiss the prophetic by defining it as merely preaching. Others wish to eliminate any fortune-telling and so define prophecy as only forth telling of God's already written word. Actually all must admit the same fact : Strong's # **G4395** προφητεύω prophēteuō *prof-ate-yoo'-o* from G4396; to *foretell* events, *divine, speak* under *inspiration, exercise* the prophetic *office:* - prophesy.

Further, the context clearly suggests that people, indeed both the non-ordained and women where speaking under divine inspiration and not only edifying the church but also convicting sinners. When Paul says in I Corinthians 12:1, that he wouldn't have us ignorant of "spiritual *things*" **G4152** νευματικός pneumatikos *phyoo-mat-ik-os'* it is abundantly clear that he has in mind supernatural manifestations. Thus, as much as I would also like to limit aberrations of good order, I can not go along with throwing out manifestations of Holy Spirit that we are commanded to pursue!

Clearly Paul's aim in writing is to respond to questions and by his answers increase proper order – with no lessening of ardor for the Lord and the advancement of the mission. This is also my aim in writing. We can be ecstatically grateful that indeed God does speak to us. We can be wonderfully grateful that God speaks to us all. We can be humble and diligent to listen. We can aspire to being honored to be a mail carrier. And that is enough.

If we agree that there are supernatural manifestations of God speaking in various ways to anyone, let's admit that this is not preaching. We don't need a law like the Clarendon Code (a law in England in John Wesley's day that limited who could preach) to realize that not just anyone can or should preach, but only those recognized by the church and ideally trained, with something to say, and with a model life. But we all can say what we are hearing from God. God once used a donkey. Thank goodness!

Sometimes there is an element of foretelling, or talking about the future, in some of these messages. How could we make a rule on God that God can't mention anything future? Prophecy is not, however, fortune-telling, augury, or some sort of Christian divination. Instead, it is carrying mail. God does the talking and we all agree that God is not mentally ill; God speaks in a manner that is congruent with Scripture. And with good doctrine and other true prophecies.

Further, today's prophecy is not like Old Testament prophets in that it does supersede but is ruled by canon (the Bible) and doesn't become canon (rule of faith and practice as is the Bible.) Indeed Paul wants to make sure that even in the early church, no one could come up with something wild. That is why he says "and the other prophets judge." Also, we can tell that both Paul and the folks to whom he was writing were using the Torah (law in Scripture) as a reference for what was correct.

So I have eliminated the 3 fears that make people want to eliminate prophecy: it can not over-rule Scripture, it is not fortune-telling, and we must admit and allow God speaking to everyone today. However, let's talk a bit more about preaching. While prophecy is not simply preaching, preaching ideally should be prophetic. Surely you have heard preachers who indicate that their message was given to them by God; that say "God seems to want me to say this today." Further, you have heard people say, "Wow that was really meant for me today!" If not, go elsewhere. Do not, however, be misled that prophecy is anything other than what is face value indicated: a supernatural manifestation of God speaking to people.

Another thing that people get tied in knots about is the difference between anyone who might prophesy and someone who holds the office of a prophet. I've seen articulated classification systems! Where is this in Scripture? Greek definition seems to rule it out. Why such a big deal about this? Perhaps pulling rank. Perhaps a fear of disorder. Why don't we just talk about good church order? Later we will consider what being a prophet means and entails and the most important point of church order in reference to our topic: how a prophet (or one who prophesies) should interface with a pastor.

Correct church order, as laid out in Ephesians 4:11 includes the 4 or 5 ministries: apostles (those given special assignments for churches or movements) prophets (those who are recognized by the church as bringers of God's special words), evangelists, and pastors and teachers. Some people count pastor/teacher as one office. The argument for this comes from the Greek because the word *some* is missing before *teacher*, so the text may be read as "and some as pastors and teachers." However, I do understand those that teach in the church, as a Sunday School teacher, to be important enough to vet, train, and recognize. Further, school teachers and professors in Christian schools are extensions of ministry. John Calvin called professors "doctors of the church, envisioning teachers as an extension of the church. In such cases surely they also ought to be required to live and teach at a high standard and be given great honor. In the situation of secular governments today, we cannot make a rule that all teachers are employees of the church, but the principle of teachers being moral paragons and purveyors of Truth nevertheless is the ideal. Certainly, the 4 or 5 are specified, and while the old paradigm of the one pastor, possibly under a bishop, and helped by a music person is still the norm, the vision of a 5 fold ministry is blooming. While we will make some comments about experiences in a more 4 or 5 fold paradigm, most of our focus will be on how a prophet should conduct her or himself with the pastor of the local congregation. Our point here is to recognize that prophets being in the church is specified as proper order.

Now, much has been said about gifts as opposed to offices and some have laid out great patterns for levels of offices. This I do not find in the Bible. It is certainly possible that one may offer a gift without being someone who is recognized as regularly doing so. However, anyone who prophesies regularly, and with recognition from other prophets and the clergy, normally the pastor of their congregation, is obviously a prophet. Further, someone who functions at the congregational level, may not be someone who functions at a conference or national level, let alone travels as a prophet. Even people who are stage level prophets may not be gifted and called to prophesy national future warnings. Others may – who don't even look like a prophet in the religious sense. So, empirically, we might acknowledge that there seems to be levels of work (just are there are of levels of preaching/pastoring/presiding. However, getting into delineating levels, let alone enforcing such levels seems like at the very least a distraction, and possibly a temptation to over-lording or grasping at power. A better aim would be to ensure that we have prophetic words that are really from God, and the way to do that is clearly stated in I Corinthians, especially 14: 29 "that the other prophets judge" and clearly to be in order. If everyone is focused on hearing from the Lord, then all questions of place and rank fall away. God can tell people when and how to deliver words, and the Bible tells us to use good sense and deference in delivery. So a good prophet will carry mail in the time and place s/he is assigned to do, and not impose upon a gathering or level where s/he is not.

This should be our first point: let's seek the gifts, for the sake of others connecting to God. Yes, for sure, let's seek to prophesy. Let's pray that we interpret. Let's pursue all the gifts. Anyone who aspires to an office, similarly, aspires to a good work. So, stop. Are we doing that? If not, let's right now turn and start.

Our second greatest point is let's use the gifts correctly, to strengthen everyone's connection to God. Notice that Corinthians clearly says that all the gifts are for the building up of the entire body, and so does the Ephesians 4. We are to grow up the individuals and the group, toward being like Jesus. Gifts and offices are not for self aggrandizement, nor for status, and certainly not for over-lording. If used for keeping people down, it is like seething a kid in its mother's milk or purposely stunting a child: horrible. If used for money, it is courting disaster. God showed Simon the Sorcerer (Acts 8) great and immediate judgment when after all, it seems to me that he had very little way of knowing that his request was wrong. You, dear reader, by contrast, if you have been a Christian any length of time, and probably such is the case if you aspire to any such office as prophet, you know very well that neither gift nor office is for money or honor for one's flesh. Let's have some fear of God.

It is like Mother is making a great dinner party and we get to help set the table, but we should realize that the dishes we are carrying are very valuable, so let's do not fear to carry them, but let's do it with attention and diligence.

For more consideration of this topic, let us turn to our only rule of faith and practice, the inerrant word of God.

2 Accept Bible Clarity About Gifts, Character, Order

May I say to you that the Bible is fairly clear in talking about gifts, character and order. While it might not have everything we want to know about everything we face today, what is does say on this these topics is fairly clear. May I say to you that the problems often arise Both from not knowing the words and not accepting the clarity?

1Co 12:1 Now concerning spiritual *gifts,* brethren, I would not have you ignorant.

I would like to call for a coming together of learning and hearing, so that we are less ignorant of spiritual things. This manual is my current contribution. We should be assured that the Spirit speaks with one voice and is not schizoid or schizophrenic. God will make sense (even if occasionally being above our original understanding.) God is a communicative God and wants to communicate to us, to lift us up. All our hearing in prayer and worship, and prophetic gifts will certainly match with Scripture. Scholar and mystic may reside in the same person and should reside in the same congregation, and at their heights in movements and one day in the wider church. Scholar and mystic can come together. We must shake off the laziness that is upon us from the wider culture and we must shake off the two-ness, some being of heart and hearing and others of Scripture and head. We should not be ignorant.

1Co 12:2 Ye know that ye were Gentiles, carried away unto these dumb idols, even as ye were led.

1Co 12:3 Wherefore I give you to understand, that no man speaking by the Spirit of God calleth Jesus accursed: and *that* no man can say that Jesus is the Lord, but by the Holy Ghost.

All will be done to glorify Jesus, and Jesus will be Lord of our doings.

1Co 12:4 Now there are diversities of gifts, but the same Spirit.

1Co 12:5 And there are differences of administrations, but the same Lord.

1Co 12:6 And there are diversities of operations, but it is the same God which worketh all in all.

1Co 12:7 But the manifestation of the Spirit is given to every man to profit withal.

1Co 12:8 For to one is given by the Spirit the word of wisdom; to another the word of knowledge by the same Spirit;

1Co 12:9 To another faith by the same Spirit; to another the gifts of healing by the same Spirit;

1Co 12:10 To another the working of miracles; to another prophecy; to another discerning of spirits; to another *divers* kinds of tongues; to another the interpretation of tongues:

1Co 12:11 But all these worketh that one and the selfsame Spirit, dividing to every man severally as he will.

1Co 12:12 For as the body is one, and hath many members, and all the members of that one body, being many, are one body: so also *is* Christ.

1Co 12:13 For by one Spirit are we all baptized into one body, whether *we be* Jews or Gentiles, whether *we be* bond or free; and have been all made to drink into one Spirit.

1Co 12:14 For the body is not one member, but many.

1Co 12:15 If the foot shall say, Because I am not the hand, I am not of the body; is it therefore not of the body?

1Co 12:16 And if the ear shall say, Because I am not the eye, I am not of the body; is it therefore not of the body?

1Co 12:17 If the whole body *were* an eye, where *were* the hearing? If the whole *were* hearing, where *were* the smelling?

1Co 12:18 But now hath God set the members every one of them in the body, as it hath pleased him.

1Co 12:19 And if they were all one member, where *were* the body?

1Co 12:20 But now *are they* many members, yet but one body.

1Co 12:21 And the eye cannot say unto the hand, I have no need of thee: nor again the head to the feet, I have no need of you.

1Co 12:22 Nay, much more those members of the body, which seem to be more feeble, are necessary:

1Co 12:23 And those *members* of the body, which we think to be less honourable, upon these we bestow more abundant honour; and our uncomely *parts* have more abundant comeliness.

1Co 12:24 For our comely *parts* have no need: but God hath tempered the body together, having given more abundant honour to that *part* which lacked:

1Co 12:25 That there should be no schism in the body; but *that* the members should have the same care one for another.

1Co 12:26 And whether one member suffer, all the members suffer with it; or one member be honoured, all the members rejoice with it.

1Co 12:27 Now ye are the body of Christ, and members in particular.

I Co 12:28 And God hath set some in the church, first apostles, secondarily prophets, thirdly teachers, after that miracles, then gifts of healings, helps, governments, diversities of tongues.

1Co 12:29 *Are* all apostles? *are* all prophets? *are* all teachers? *are* all workers of miracles?

1Co 12:30 Have all the gifts of healing? do all speak with tongues? do all interpret?

1Co 12:31 But covet earnestly the best gifts: and yet shew I unto you a more excellent way.

The most important point here is that gifts are given to profit the whole body. Therefore, they are not to exalt one member, nor to divide the body. Further, notice that Paul does not make a big division of gifts on one side and offices on the other, as he talks about setting in some in positions and then returns to mention gifts. It is permissible for us to think of them separately, but because of this passage and how Paul deals with it, as well as my observation, that people who regularly and with recognition use the gift of prophecy are thereby prophets. This is not to say that they are necessarily national level, Old Testament, stage performance type prophets, just as the average pastor is not a national figure. So as a pastor normally serves in a local congregation, I call such prophets, "house prophets." Everyone has their current level of assignment. Once again, the point is to edify the rest of the body, not to make levels, ranks, and over-lords. Do you see that here we have one thought? The pastor of a very large congregation is thankful for the folks who clean the bathroom, so that people aren't distracted by stink. He is thankful for the soundmen who make it so he can be heard and the day is celebrative rather than annoying. The Mega-Church Pastor is so precisely because he can handle so many other people doing so many other things. Because he has mastered administration as well as preaching, he has a bigger spot. Nevertheless, some pastors in smaller churches are good pastors, saints of God, and maybe be will receive a greater crown. It is not about spot; it is all about the Body, receiving the Word of the Spirit. It is about Jesus and the Bride loving.

Do not be unhappy with your place in the body. Those who are given greater gifts and greater offices suffer more. If you do desire a greater gifts and greater office, you do well, and will obtain if you both listen to God and aim at serving others in love. There is the frustration: wanting more without love, for in these cases you will be blocked, if not by the Spirit, certainly by people. And there is persecution. And there might be God's timing, but usually that is not nearly as slow as big-mouthed controllers in the church make it out to be. Just ask if you need to grow or rest, and if God says "go for it," then do.

1Co 12:1 But covet earnestly the best gifts: and yet shew I unto you a more excellent way.

Please notice Paul's seque. He goes on to talk about love being more important than gifts, martyrdom and so forth, but those who wish to deny gifts must excise the first half of the sentence: "Covet the best gifts." The word for "covet earnestly" is *zeloo* in Greek, which you probably immediately recognize as the root word for "zealous." Strong's Exhaustive Concordance says it means: have a warmth of feeling for. It is translated in the King James as be envious of, jealous of, or zealously affected for.

I Co 12:1 But earnestly desire the greater gifts. NASB

But earnestly desire *and* strive for the greater gifts [if acquiring them is going to be your goal]. *Amplified*

But be zealous-for[aj] the greater gifts. Disciples New Literal

But strive[s] for the greater gifts. And I will show you a still more excellent way. *Lexham Enlgish*

Now eagerly desire the greater gifts. NIV

and desire earnestly the better gifts; and yet a far excelling way do I shew to you: *Youngs' Literal*

It's obvious by now, isn't it, that Christ's church is a complete Body and not a gigantic, uni-dimensional Part? It's not all Apostle, not all Prophet, not all Miracle Worker, not all Healer, not all Prayer in Tongues, not all Interpreter of Tongues. And yet some of you keep competing for so-called "important" parts. *Message*

Notice that the Message is not a translation, and is on the minority report side. I checked and the Greek is *Znloute,* a command.

So here it is completely literal, from Berry's *Interlinear*:

I Co 12:1 Be emulous of be the gifts better, and yet more surpassing a way to you I show.

So Paul's overall point in the 12th chapter is to earnestly desire gifts in order to build up the whole body (not just yourself.) Then in the second half of the sentence, he makes a transition to what is now our 13th Chapter about love. A face value reading says nothing whatsoever to deny what is said in the 12th and 14th chapters, although many with straight face will argue that it does. This would make Paul a schizophrenic and the Spirit untrustworthy. That the Spirit of Jesus Christ works somehow differently now than in the Apostolic age is just a story repeated by people who were too afraid, doubting, or lazy to be obedient to the clear words of Scripture. Let's see what chapter 14 says.

1Co 14:1 Follow after charity, and desire spiritual *gifts,* but rather that ye may prophesy. KJV

Pursue love, and be emulous of spirituals, but rather that ye may prophesy. Berry's *Interlinear*

Yes, a chapter on love is certainly requisite and salutary right here in the smack dab middle of instructions on spiritual gifts, and those of you who are used to the bursting forth, the blossoming, and unsure steps along with the Jezebels, Absaloms, and unclean spirits (attracted like flies to old meat) surely know that this is good advice. Character is more important than gifts. We should strive to add character to our salvation by grace, see 2 Peter 1:5 -8 and that point is made many other places. It is a point that needs to be focused upon much more these days, when right and wrong has been forgotten. Today, when we have congregations focused each on a certain aspect, with one on Reformed doctrine and history and government, and the one down the street on getting people saved, and the one around the corner on spiritual gifts, we should remember that this is one whole thing. Our use of the gifts will go much better if we comport ourselves with Christ-like character. We will find ourselves better led if we install leaders on the basis of both anointing and character – not on potential and a gift and certainly not on looks, promotion, or education alone – and thereby end up with someone who looks good and is easily turned in a wrong direction.

1Co 13:1 Though I speak with the tongues of men and of angels, and have not charity, I am become *as* sounding brass, or a tinkling cymbal.

1Co 13:2 And though I have *the gift of* prophecy, and understand all
mysteries, and all knowledge; and though I have all faith, so that I
could remove mountains, and have not charity, I am nothing.

1Co 13:3 And though I bestow all my goods to feed *the poor,* and though
I give my body to be burned, and have not charity, it profiteth me
nothing.

So a strong gift of speaking in tongues, the gift of prophecy,
the talent of great scholarship, the gift of faith of the strongest kind
of miracles are all alike nothing without agape love. Even
martyrdom would count for nothing if not for love. Has knowledge
passed away? Is martyrdom for the faith not honorable today?
Then how can one do violence to the text and suggest that gifts are
somehow here denied?

1Co 13:4 Charity suffereth long, *and* is kind; charity envieth not; charity
vaunteth not itself, is not puffed up,

1Co 13:5 Doth not behave itself unseemly, seeketh not her own, is not
easily provoked, thinketh no evil;

1Co 13:6 Rejoiceth not in iniquity, but rejoiceth in the truth;

1Co 13:7 Beareth all things, believeth all things, hopeth all things,
endureth all things.

1Co 13:8 Charity never faileth:

Here agape love is characterized. Notice, at the top of the list is
"suffereth long." You will find that in the use of gifts, we must be
patient. Notice that, as I have said, gifts and office are not for self-
aggrandizement – even though you may find successful mentors
who require it of you and even though it does seem like it is
necessary. Notice that we should hope the best of others (and so
my brother's word on being encouraging and what I take his
intentions to be may stem from this. We are not told the dirt on
someone to spew dirt around, but with the aim of restoring and
improve our sibling.)

1Co 13:8 Charity never faileth: but whether *there be* prophecies,
they shall fail; whether *there be* tongues, they shall cease;
whether *there be* knowledge, it shall vanish away.

1Co 13:9 For we know in part, and we prophesy in part.

1Co 13:10 But when that which is perfect is come, then that which is in part shall be done away.

1Co 13:11 When I was a child, I spake as a child, I understood as a child, I thought as a child: but when I became a man, I put away childish things.

1Co 13:12 For now we see through a glass, darkly; but then face to face: now I know in part; but then shall I know even as also I am known.

1Co 13:13 And now abideth faith, hope, charity, these three; but the greatest of these *is* charity

Nothing here mentions the Bible, as if Scripture did not exist then. Nothing here wipes out both 12th and 14th chapter. Yes, our gifts are not perfect because they come through us, human beings. One day Christ will return, all things will be gathered up in Him, and He will give it all to the Father. By that standard, all we do is frail, passing, and will then be past. Then we will know all. But wait, aren't these gifts *manifestations of the Spirit*? Wait, don't we "know all" (I John 2:20)? I can understand what my non-charismatic brothers are saying, but strict adherence to Scripture seems to indicate a more optimistic view. Indeed the spiritual experience may indeed be an important part of our *telos*, our end point of becoming more like Christ.

Now, having said this, I too am of the opinion that the canon is closed and all prophecy must come under the rule of Scripture. Anyone who thinks he can leave the Bible behind thinks of himself higher than Jesus did of Himself. Jesus fulfilled Scripture, and quoted it. Although, granted, His understanding was so superior to others that they were often amazed, nevertheless, He was in line with it. As said before, the Spirit speaks with one voice. Thus, we will go down the road, not falling into the ditch of denying gifts which we are commanded to pursue and not getting so involved in spiritual gifts that we forget Giver, more sure Word, and purpose of them.

1Co 14:1 Follow after charity, and desire spiritual *gifts,* but rather that ye may prophesy.

1Co 14:2 For he that speaketh in an *unknown* tongue speaketh not unto men, but unto God: for no man understandeth *him;* howbeit in the spirit he speaketh mysteries.

1Co 14:3 But he that prophesieth speaketh unto men *to* edification, and exhortation, and comfort.

1Co 14:4 He that speaketh in an *unknown* tongue edifieth himself; but he that prophesieth edifieth the church.

1Co 14:5 I would that ye all spake with tongues, but rather that ye prophesied: for greater *is* he that prophesieth than he that speaketh with tongues, except he interpret, that the church may receive edifying.

1Co 14:6 Now, brethren, if I come unto you speaking with tongues, what shall I profit you, except I shall speak to you either by revelation, or by knowledge, or by prophesying, or by doctrine?

1Co 14:7 And even things without life giving sound, whether pipe or harp, except they give a distinction in the sounds, how shall it be known what is piped or harped?

1Co 14:8 For if the trumpet give an uncertain sound, who shall prepare himself to the battle?

1Co 14:9 So likewise ye, except ye utter by the tongue words easy to be understood, how shall it be known what
is spoken? for ye shall speak into the air.

1Co 14:10 There are, it may be, so many kinds of voices in the world, and none of them *is* without signification.

1Co 14:11 Therefore if I know not the meaning of the voice, I shall be unto him that speaketh a barbarian, and he that speaketh *shall be* a barbarian unto me.

1Co 14:12 Even so ye, forasmuch as ye are zealous of spiritual *gifts,* seek that ye may excel to the edifying of the church.

1Co 14:13 Wherefore let him that speaketh in an *unknown* tongue pray that he may interpret.

1Co 14:14 For if I pray in an *unknown* tongue, my spirit prayeth, but my understanding is unfruitful.

1Co 14:15 What is it then? I will pray with the spirit, and I will pray with the understanding also: I will sing with the spirit, and I will sing with the understanding also.

1Co 14:16 Else when thou shalt bless with the spirit, how shall he that occupieth the room of the unlearned say Amen at thy giving of thanks, seeing he understandeth not what thou sayest?

1Co 14:17 For thou verily givest thanks well, but the other is not edified.

1Co 14:18 I thank my God, I speak with tongues more than ye all:

1Co 14:19 Yet in the church I had rather speak five words with my understanding, that *by my voice* I might teach others also, than ten thousand words in an *unknown* tongue.

1Co 14:20 Brethren, be not children in understanding: howbeit in malice be ye children, but in understanding be men.

1Co 14:21 In the law it is written, With *men of* other tongues and other lips will I speak unto this people; and yet for all that will they not hear me, saith the Lord.

In the 14th verse Paul clearly lays out distinctions and balance, that had been directly attacked by popular interpretation. Why is it so difficult to take Scripture at face value? Particular by those who claim they believe the maps and cover? Of course, generally, we should all speak in tongues. Obviously we are going to speak the common language, mostly, when we gather. Obviously we are going to want to hear God at all times, and of course share when we are together. Obviously the God is a God of the supernatural. Certainly, this have been the experience of the people of God since the dawn of recorded history. So what is the problem? Maybe prideful intellecutalism? You think? Once again Paul clearly, insistently, and strongly urges that we pursue spiritual gifts zealously for the building up of others.

14 Pursue love, yet desire earnestly spiritual *gifts*, but especially that you may prophesy. NASB

14 Pursue [this] love [with eagerness, make it your goal], yet earnestly desire *and* cultivate the spiritual *gifts* [to be used by believers for the benefit of the church], but especially that you may prophesy [to foretell the future, to speak a new message from God to the people] *Amplified*

Be pursuing love.

Now be zealous-for the spiritual *gifts*, but even-more that you might be prophesying. *Disciples Literal New Testament*

14 Pursue love, and desire spiritual gifts, but especially the gift of speaking what God has revealed. *God's Word Translation*

14 1a Follow, then, the way of love, while you set your heart on the gifts of the Spirit.
1b-4 The highest gift you can wish for is to be able to speak the messages of God. *Phillip's*

14 Follow the way of love and eagerly desire gifts of the Spirit, especially prophecy. NIV

14 So *in everything* strive to love. Passionately seek the gifts of the Spirit, especially the gift of prophecy. *The Voice*

14 Follow ye charity, love ye spiritual things, but more that ye prophesy. *Wycliffe*

14 Pursue the love, and seek earnestly the spiritual things, and rather that ye may prophecy, *Young's Literal*

Really, that is rather clear, isn't it? We have a big enough challenge in the doing, so let's hear and understand

3 Paul's Church Order

Paul has said strongly that he wants the gifts sought after in Chapter 12 and especially asks his readers to seek to prophesy, and then he places love as an even higher standard in Chapter 13, and then in Chapter 14 he talks about church order. Is this not obvious that Paul is continuing on in the same thought as in chapter 12? This chapter, however, he takes up prophetic order. He compares prophecy with the gift of tongues and interpretation and how sharing these is to be done in order in the church meetings.

Obviously Paul is glad his readers speak in tongues and he clearly says that he speaks in tongues more than they do. So clearly tongues is honored. Specifically he says that tongues must be appropriate prayer, since the Spirit prays it. Wonderful gift to have perfect prayer, even when one has no idea how to pray! Let's not neglect that!

Incidentally, I have heard two national level ministers say that praying a lot in tongues is/was their key to success. One prayed in tongues steady for days until he was given blueprints and anointing to start his church, which became very large and is now more like a denomination. Another says he prays in tongues and walks around ignorant and blind and great things just fall on him. He urges everyone to pray at least 10 minutes a day in tongues. Studies show that most don't. Okay, stop right now and pray in tongues!

1Co 14:22 Wherefore tongues are for a sign, not to them that believe, but to them that believe not: but prophesying *serveth* not for them that believe not, but for them which believe.

In this verse Paul says that tongues are for a sign to unbelievers. I deduce then that people were speaking in tongues in the meetings, for this is the context of the chapter, and not in private only. To order tongues to be in private only, then to me seems like a variety of forbidding tongues. However, I do agree that all things be done decently and in order and there are many times and places where tongues blurted out to interrupt would be disorderly. But tongues prayed personally during a worship service where amplified music is the norm can hardly be forbidden. Certainly it has been the dearly held custom in pentecostal churches to have certain occasions when the pastor prays in tongues for a short time, and this has never been disorderly, but considered instructive, inspirational leadership. Further, singing in tongues by the congregation all together is really wonderful. In any case, there must be some tongues somewhere around in public meetings, or this verse makes no sense.

It is reasonable to think that sure, because these are meetings of believers and because believers believe, that prophecy would of course be mostly for them. I do know of times where prophecy has been given that was a sign to unbelievers, but this sort would might not be appropriate for a public meeting. For instance, imagine a famous international prophet prophesying in a service. Who would listen, believers or non-believers? Then imagine anyone giving a personal word to an unbeliever that would be such that they would fall down on their knees repenting. Probably that would be too personal to be done in a service. Preaching, by contrast, might be such. We had that in previous revivals; may we have that again. At any rate, let me not tie God's hands!

1Co 14:23 If therefore the whole church be come together into one place, and all speak with tongues, and there come in *those that are* unlearned, or unbelievers, will they not say that ye are mad?

1Co 14:24 But if all prophesy, and there come in one that believeth not, or *one* unlearned, he is convinced of all, he is judged of all:

1Co 14:25 And thus are the secrets of his heart made manifest; and so falling down on *his* face he will worship God, and report that God is in you of a truth.

From these verses we do see the gifts in operation for evangelistic purposes. I'd like to see this in practice in the church, but we do see this in operation outside the church, in such places as the mall, fair, and park. Nothing forbids taking the gifts out into the market place for evangelism, but still I would urge people go two-by-two. For a long while I hesitated, because I was so strong on "let the other prophets judge" and was so disturbed by the disorder of "ladies bathroom prophecy." However, given now some years of seeing the method of evangelism based on offering prayer for people and getting healings, based on gifts of knowledge and likely on prophecy, without hearing of disorder, I can hardly speak against it. It would seem that the prophetic should naturally go with us everywhere we go. Firstly, going two by two does permit a check and balance of judgment. Secondly, nothing in the practice directs the church. Thirdly, I am assuming that the Christians here are not being rude, but in good order for the time, place, and culture in which they are ministering. And fourthly, I would assume that they are using the gift of prophecy in a context-appropriate way. Normally, it would be ridiculous to go out and shout "Thus saith the Lord" to a person who didn't know you, although one might say that preaching on some street corners. When doing one-on-one evangelism, probably one is saying, "Gosh, I feel like maybe you are ......" Maybe even, "I really think God is telling me that..." Given my experience and typical situations, I think this sort of spirit and words would be effective and others not. If someone else's practice differs, then the proof is in the pudding. Situations differ greatly. Anyway, in this passage, we see that gifts are to be used for evangelism as well as edification of the church.

1Co 14:26 How is it then, brethren? when ye come together, every one of you hath a psalm, hath a doctrine, hath a tongue, hath a revelation, hath an interpretation. Let all things be done unto edifying.

1Co 14:27 If any man speak in an *unknown* tongue, *let it be* by two, or at the most *by* three, and *that* by course; and let one interpret.

1Co 14:28 But if there be no interpreter, let him keep silence in the church; and let him speak to himself, and to God.

1Co 14:29 Let the prophets speak two or three, and let the other judge.

1Co 14:30 If *any thing* be revealed to another that sitteth by, let the first hold his peace.

1Co 14:31 For ye may all prophesy one by one, that all may learn, and all may be comforted.

1Co 14:32 And the spirits of the prophets are subject to the prophets.

1Co 14:33 For God is not *the author* of confusion, but of peace, as in all churches of the saints.

From these texts we see that participative worship is expected. Further, we see than an orderliness is expected. We see that Paul expects a limit. We see that carriers may be in situations where they must choose to be quiet.

It is my experience that when the spirit of prophesy moves, I feel it, even when I am not the one given the prophecy. In places where there are many who prophecy, it has felt like a wave through the congregation. I remember one convention service where the Spirit was moving and many prophesied in turn. Some people got on and rode their surfboard in order to show off. After a while, it is too much for the congregation to digest. I figure that is why Paul says 2 or 3.

Given what I have seen as churches embark on use of the gifts, verse 29 is very important. There must be a covering in the congregation (or conference) such that any prophecy that is amiss may be corrected and any prophet who is acting as a false prophet is corrected, improved, or shut up. While in most cases correction of someone is not in public, for the congregation, there needs to be a clear understanding of what is taught in that house.

I was in a denomination once where there was never any public correction of preaching. Things were often as clear as mud. After 40 years, only the most twisted stuff remains. Most have left. What is taught now is often opposite to what the founders taught. There must always be a central, agreed upon central doctrine in any ongoing group.

For newbies just learning to prophesy, of course, one does not correct harshly. I am reminded of Becky Fischer who leads children into hear from the Lord. She says to children, "Now is that what you think the Lord would say? Let's listen again." Normally they correct themselves.

Indeed, once I saw in a church a person training for the ministry, teaching Sunday School, make a mistake in what she was teaching. The pastor later, in the service, almost certainly with no way of knowing what had previously been said, but probably preaching prophetically, took up the same topic and set it right. Although the trainee was embarrassed, it is likely that very few actually caught what was going on. Both clarity and charity reigned in that congregation.

There will always be one person who is presiding at the meeting, someone recognized by the church. They can close the meeting with friendly words that will return clarity. In dangerous cases, where something crazy has been said, the presiding officer, at the close of the meeting could say something like, "Let's all remember that we believe ... quote Bible passage... and thank you and good night." This is enough to erase the rare harmful thing.

Further, every group should have a culture of "in authority [by being] under authority." We all submit to the authority of Christ when we become born again; we all defer to one another. We all serve in an office only because we do so as a servant of God. We all have authority in our job only because we represent the company and are doing what our boss tells us to do. Every elected official has power only because the election vested it in him or her. It is no different in the church. We have authority only inasmuch as we are under the authority of Christ and His representatives in the church. People disrespectful of congregational authority, normally the pastor, are out of order. Similarly, no pastor should permit a false prophet to continue in his congregation. Jezebels arise only where Ahabs permit; Absaloms arise only where David has been slack. Any congregation that does not have a culture of deference and a healthy respect for authority has bigger and more pressing problems than only the prophetic, and should go back to the Word of God. Of course, it is possible to over-do this, too. Incidentally, studies do show that congregational systems that are more Bible-based tend to be healthier than those which are not. Problems in congregational culture may indeed surface through the prophetic, but the answer is not to suppress Holy Spirit, but to listen more closely, first to the written Word and then also to the prophetic words.

4 Women's Contributions Welcome

Now here is the passage you thought I would omit. I don't think so. Let's talk about this. Here is how the King James Version renders it:

1Co 14:34 Let your women keep silence in the churches: for it is not permitted unto them to speak; but *they are commanded* to be under obedience, as also saith the law.

1Co 14:35 And if they will learn any thing, let them ask their husbands at home: for it is a shame for women to speak in the church.

1Co 14:36 What? came the word of God out from you? or came it unto you only?

1Co 14:37 If any man think himself to be a prophet, or spiritual, let him acknowledge that the things that I write unto you are the commandments of the Lord.

1Co 14:38 But if any man be ignorant, let him be ignorant.

We owe a huge debt of gratitude to our English speaking forerunners who worked, suffered, and died to bring us, the common people, the Word of God. We thank those on the translating team of King James the I of England! Wycliffe and Tyndale even more. These men gave their lives. My ancestor, named Lively, was on the translating team and had to flee to Ulster because he miscalculated just how Protestant King James I was. King James had the Bible translated, not just to keep order, but to protect his monarchy, by suppressing the Geneva Bible, that was republican rather than monarchical. Remember that Jacobean England was a long time ago. They did not have good understanding of ancient manuscripts. Even Hebrew to them was a dead language. Further, they had prejudices that entered into their translation. This I say because it is true. We are immensely blessed by how much King James Bible language entered into English, and we are also blessed today by much greater access through more manuscripts, better translations, more understanding of Hebrew and Hebrew culture, and the possibility of greater learning.

The first rule of Bible exegesis is comparing Scripture with Scripture. So first let us note that Paul in I Corinthians 11: 5 indicates that women were praying and prophesying in public meetings. It is tempting to go into great exegesis of this and other passage relating to women, but let's try to focus on the task at hand. (I will recommend two books: 1) *Woman in the Church* by Russel C. Prohl (Missouri Synod Lutheran professor, Eerdmans 1957, and 2) *Priscilla's Letter* by Ruth Hoppin, Lost Coast Press, 2009.) Given that the same author, Paul, in the same epistle, I Corinthians, talks about how women should pray and prophesy in public, it makes no sense that he forbids it here.

The second and third rule of Bible exegesis is to interpret in historical and grammatical context. Since Jews in synagogues then and the most conservative Jews even today, sit with men and women separated, and since in those days Jewish men were taught to read and taught Torah while most women were illiterate and not taught Torah, it made sense that women shouldn't be shouting across the room to ask husbands a question. It is for this reason that the Message translates the passage this way:

I Co 14:34-36 Wives must not disrupt worship, talking when they should be listening, asking questions that could more appropriately be asked of their husbands at home. God's Book of the Law guides our manners and customs here. Wives have no license to use the time of worship for unwarranted speaking. Do you—both women *and* men—imagine that you're a sacred oracle determining what's right and wrong? Do you think everything revolves around you? *Message*

This reading makes sense in context too, because Paul is talking about keeping order. Clearly even this brings up a question to people who think this text forbids women's leadership: did they read this verse with that interpretation because *a priori* they assumed that women can't be trained, ordained, and representing the church?

However, in any case, today we know more about the text, the times, and Jewish customs. Even without such knowledge, if we pay very close attention to the text, we discover something that overturns our first reading with English eyes.

34 Women should keep quiet in the church meetings. They are not allowed to speak, but they must yield to this rule as the law says. *New Century*

34 The women are to keep silent in the churches; for they are not permitted to speak, but are to subject themselves, just as the Law also says. NASB

34 let the women be silent in the churches. For it is not permitted *for* them to speak]. But let them be subject, just as the Law also says. *Disciples Literal New Testament*

34 Your women in the assemblies let them be silent, for it hath not been permitted to them to speak, but to be subject, as also the law saith; *Wycliffe*

Did you see it? The Law never says for women to keep silent. Never. By contrast, we see Deborah as a good judge, Huldah as a prophetess that is consulted by leaders, and Esther who is commanded to speak to the Emperor, even without a summons. Further, the Risen Christ sent Mary Magdalene as the first proclaimer of his resurrection to his apostles. Clearly women were traveling in the company with Jesus, although in that age they could hardly be sent out, not only for culture's sake, but also because there was no contraception so they were busy having babies. Paul has no problem going to Lydia's prayer meeting. Notice, importantly, that Paul greets an apostle named Junias, a woman's name (Romans 16:6). Further, from a close reading of Hebrews, one sees that it was Priscilla who wrote it. I hear people foolishly say, interrupting their preaching, saying that they believe Paul wrote Hebrews! Could it have been Paul who says in self-effacing manner "submit to the elders" and "I know you will be patient with me for exhorting you"? No! Paul says takes authority saying, "Paul, an apostle".... and a variety of "you elders smarten up." Further, Paul and any Jew would have difficulty saying that the Altar of Incense was in the Holiest of Holies (Hb 9:3 &4). Furthermore, Paul just does not write such glorious Greek – except in certain places. Scholars suggest that maybe Priscilla edited Paul. She certainly would have been in a position to do so as a daughter of a Roman senator who hosted both Peter and Paul, and who later led congregations, as we know by archeological evidence. By the way, why in the world would anyone have stripped off the authorship if it were Paul? Just read Hebrews. Then, after you read Ruth Hoppin's book, I think you will kick yourself for not reading Hebrews more closely.

In this passage in I Cor 4:29, Paul is quoting the question that he got (cf. I Cor 7:1). Someone in Corinth argued that these women should be quiet. Paul already says that women should pray and prophesy in public, although with their veils on, so not to look as if they were prostitutes. Probably they were comporting themselves as if the meeting were a private gathering and Paul urges them to think of it as a public gathering for missionary and evangelism reasons, not to look licentious to outsiders. Further, wives are in subjection to husbands, not as *archon*/rulers but as *kephale*/sources. So be smart and cooperate with your financial source. That makes sense even today. But nowhere are women told to generally keep silent in the Torah, and it doesn't make sense to think it does here.

Here, to take this as a prohibition, one must swallow an assertion contrary to fact (about what Torah says) -- or assert that

Paul is ignorant of the Law, which is silly. Certainly one should not interrupt a preacher to ask a question. One does so during a lecture, only upon invitation. Even less would it be proper decorum in worship. We agree on this. So the Message interpretation, which stood for some years, may be accepted. Women should learn, however, notice. This is a huge leap from the Jewish culture of the day, that said to not teach Torah to women. Notice that Jesus did teach women, even when called out for it by Martha. In that passage, the problem Martha is complaining about was not just lack of kitchen help, but the fact that Mary was in the living room *with the men, learning Torah.* Jesus specifically permitted it. He said Mary chose the better part which would not be taken away. Hmm, maybe much like earnestly desiring the best gifts.

Jesus and Paul are great feminists. They promote women's contributions. They are not like leftists, however, who stir up strife. One offers gifts, but in an orderly way. Those who slap God's gifts away (both Spiritual manifestations and people with offices) will have something to answer for, to God Himself.

1Co 14:36 What? came the word of God out from you? or came it unto you only?

Notice Paul's next words, like "WHAT??!!" This is like the Jewish expression that is elsewhere translated "I trow not." It is like the modern, "Yeah, I don't think so" which really means "For sure no way." Paul uses this sort of expression elsewhere, such as in Galatians. The word for WHAT is an ἤ, a disjunctive particle. It could be translated, "On the contrary." So he is say, "NO! What do you think you have a corner on the truth? Do you think you are so smart? So you are the only one who hears from God?"

Do you see now, that the meaning looks a lot different than first reading from King James? I didn't get it from denying but from paying close attention to Scripture. Only the original text is inerrant, not the interpretation of 1611. Further, I compared Scripture with Scripture, and interpreted in historical and grammatical context. Not from cultural bias.

So women should learn, should pray (leading in public) and should prophesy. And no one should disrupt.

I would further mention that Paul's missionary concerns to not look bad in the wider culture still carries. Good marriages, based on the general character of men and women still makes every sense in the world. Of course, in every passage dealing with women, one must read carefully the context to determine whether Paul is talking about wives or women, because the Greek doesn't have two different words like English does. We all know that not all women are wives, and no one is a wife to all men. So let's rightly divide the Word of Truth. Okay?

1Co 14:37 If any man think himself to be a prophet, or spiritual, let him acknowledge that the things that I write unto you are the commandments of the Lord.
1Co 14:38 But if any man be ignorant, let him be ignorant.
1Co 14:39 Wherefore, brethren, covet to prophesy, and forbid not to speak with tongues.
1Co 14:40 Let all things be done decently and in order.

So Paul finishes up in his inimitable, authoritative style. His words are strong to the very person who would put down women's contribution, emphasizes orderliness, gives stern command not to forbid speaking in tongues, and harks back to his previous words in I Cor 12: that we should not be ignorant. But he evidences frustration that I too have often felt, that some people continually choose to be ignorant. However, that is not his desire. We (all of us) are to desire gifts. We are to desire to contribute to the Body and to the missionary cause of Jesus at home and abroad as much as we may, depending upon the Spirit within us.

These words from Paul, from God, then, make the foundation of any book on ordering of the prophetic.

My opinion is that it is precisely because women are so disrespected and their leadership potential so dismissed that there do arise occasions for women to lead in the prophetic that scare men, whether or not they are out of order. Training women and requiring them to submit to regular rule and then lead in regular ways cuts down on all this. Similarly, denominations where women have great leadership with women also see a lot less disorder. Let's respect "mothers in Israel" and let's respect those few women who can lead as strongly as a man. Then let men act like men and not be so weak that they can't lead unless they put down women. How about that?

5 Bible Based Advice For Today's Problems

Firstly, we should keep it clear in our hearts and minds that God wishes to speak to us and we should be diligent and grateful to hear. Secondly, we should remember that gifts and offices are not for self-aggrandizement. Rather it is about Jesus the Bridegroom passing a message to His Bride. It is about Daddy God talking with his children. It is like a sweet self-effacing mother passing on her husbands' wishes through the older children. That is how things are supposed to go. If you are not working well with you pastor, check your pride, your offense level, and how much the "accuser of the brethren" may be provoking you.

Furthermore, don't follow someone who is prophesying out of strife or for self-aggrandizement. Those called to stage ministry might have some flair that is necessary on stage, but good discernment will see a difference between leadership flair and self-interest. Flesh likes to follow pride. So check your flesh if you are following someone who is more interested in show than in Truth/glorifying Jesus/and Kingdom advancement. If you are unsure, pray for God to speak to you about the situation.

Remember that the other prophets should judge. Therefore, the prophetic is not to be done covertly. Something is extremely wrong with a person who must get you in private to "give you a word." Or gets you isolated in public and they only have control over the situation. Further, something is wrong with an experienced prophet who cannot work with others. Of course, a newby might be shy, but more experienced prophets could be encouraging. My own experience, by contrast, was not a word of encouragement, nor yet of instruction, and if you got it wrong, you got harsh correction. Well, that was okay. What is not okay is false prophets make a bad reputation for the prophetic and for the church. I am reminded of respected missionary/apostle when upon hearing about a false prophecy of when the rapture would happen that was made fun of in the press said, "I miss the Old Testament." It was a joke, of course, but the point was that false prophecies and those that make them were extremely annoying.

Please notice, this does not say, teach others for profit and get as much prophetic out, of any quality. It does say, let the other prophets judge. Of course, I am not against teachers being paid to teach, or people trying to encourage the prophetic. Rather I am aiming at eliminating the worst abuses by general knowledge so that there is more progress, for more people, more rapidly.

Shouldn't we try to do everything we do in obedience? Shouldn't we aim at the state where every word we speak is what God would have us say? So the prophetic is not limited to "prophecy" by "prophets." We know that all children of God hear God's voice.

Consequently, I would hope that most pastors would also move in spiritual things, and be one of the prophets. I would hope that most preaching is prophetic, too. Why stand up in a pulpit and say anything unless you are filled with words from the Lord? To those for whom "enthusiastic" is pejorative, let me ask you: Why would the Spirit be more likely to move you to error than human reason? Of course we should all be Biblical and all infilled by the Spirit –

ideally in all we do. Please let's help each other toward this goal; I think we are behind schedule.

Of course, we know we should do all things in order. We want to be in line with Jesus. We also need to be in reasonably in line with those who are trying to be in line with Jesus, especially when they are the recognized congregational authority. Thus we might find out how we can flow in the prophetic given the customs of the house in which we are ministering. In their own congregation, pastors may find it preferable to directly teach and publish their desires rather than cowering and hoping and fearing. Traveling ministers and local pastors should confer to whatever point they find it necessary. It is very frustrating for a traveling person to be wanting to clear something with a pastor, only to be met with disinterest, business, or aloofness, until something happens that was not discussed. Then the traveler gets the blame. No, the person who refused to communicate is at fault. Remember that when you assume…. It makes as ass out of u and me.

Special situations arise these days when a number of congregations host, visit and work together. Words get ignored and prophets get hurt or pastors scared if there are not clear rules. If the host house feels they must be responsible for all the "airtime" then they want to "know those who minister among" them so only their congregants can lead in any way. If this is the case, they should say so. If not, there should be published rules for all. I know we all hate the word *rules* but that is what they are and it makes everyone feel safer when they are published. It is frustrating no end that the "schools of the prophets" apparently never address protocol. It is short sighted and counter-productive to insist that you are the only teachers of the prophetic in town and that there were never any prophets before you showed up. Chuckle.

We can follow protocol so we know that we are not pushy and not rude, not to the house, not to the recipient and not to the Spirit. The only exception might be an apostolic or Old Testament like assignment to speak to sinners and speak against sin. These are always considered rude by people who love sin. Jeremiah was considered rude, but Nathan probably was not. If you are needing this book for guidance, then take this advice: work at not being rude. But don't judge the national level prophets based on the criticisms of unbelievers.

It is very difficult for a prophet who doesn't know the protocol in a given meeting. You might write down what you see are or what you are given and hand it up to the pastor. If you are in a situation where you are in one congregation but worshiping regularly at another, ask that other pastor, not in a public situation, how you might serve. You might for instance, be allowed to serve at the altar as a prophet, if he knows you. Some prophetically oriented houses leave a mic open for prophetic words Further, since we know that we may prophesy by turns, that the Spirit can wait for the right time, and even if you must fail to give a prophecy because of the rules or situation in the house, just look for a right way and time. Always ask the Lord for direction and ask the Spirit to cover it.

"Let the other prophets judge" means that normally use of the prophetic will be under the nose of the prophets in attendance and the pastor in charge of the local congregation. You will probably be prophesying mostly at the altar, with other prophets around. You might be given a message during a service of worship, but you will be giving this in a time that the Spirit and Pastor have provided, and not in a way to interrupt. Simply because I was around, I have even been pulled into prayer times before and after service by pastors and evangelists who wanted to be sure that their ministrations were not private. How much more should prophets be diligent for protocol.

Pastors could greatly help the situation by publishing desired protocol. I salute Pastor Kermit Bell of Glad Tidings Assembly of God, Austin, Texas for having clearly stated in the bulletin how prophetic words are to be handled in their services. In a nutshell, anyone who feels he has a prophetic message may go to him during a service (presumably sitting beside him since he sits in one of several padded chairs on the floor of the sanctuary, just off stage, in a section for the pastors) and communicate with him. He will then direct when, and presumably if, the message fits into the service. Given the likelihood of cross-visitation and electronic contingencies these days, such a thought-out protocol is almost always necessary. Why not publish it? It would relieve the prophets, reduce the fears of the leadership, and make a more open door for the Lord to speak!

Know that your aim is to build up the Body, which normally means encouraging, but also exhorting, yes? Just be diligent to pass along the mail correctly. Further, the prophetic can be used in evangelistic situations. Know too that there are varieties of expression of the prophetic. All this we deduced from the text and I hope you see how sensible it is in application to the modern situation.

6 Encouraging Words

It has been taught that only encouraging words should be given. There is an argument from I Thessalonians 5:11 that we should comfort and encourage. We do this too little. Further we might argue that we should generally encourage each other from Romans 1:12, 15:4 and I especially like Isaiah 35:3 "Encourage the exhausted, and strengthen the feeble" (all in the NSAB). More to the point for prophetic, is our text in I Co 12-14. Of course there should be no divisions, and we should show love. The most important text would be 14:3 "But the one who prophesies speak to men for edification, and exhortation, and consolation." NASB

So, yes, encouragement figures prominently, but based on the word "exhortation" there can be no prohibition against prophetic warnings. Let me say that again: no one can make a hard and fast rule that all prophecies must be encouraging. In fact, I do not think anyone ever did. I understand the rather more famous prophet who is quoted as teaching others to never prophesy anything but the encouraging to mean instead, that one need not reveal in a harsh way everything one knows. I think he meant to be diplomatic, use good judgment, and realize that some knowledge is for you rather than for sharing. For instance, if you see some sin, you don't need to be blabbing this in front of the assembled church. Maybe that was meant just as background for you to know or that you should use this knowledge in a diplomatic way. Of course, you should ask the Lord. I just can't see a general prohibition of all exhorting in all times and places. Was it wrong for Kathryn Kuhlman to call someone down for cheating in her meeting? What about the realtor who was sent back from the dead to tell his Baptist church to get right with the Lord? What are the two witness going to be saying? No, I just can't see a general, hard and fast rule for all times and places that all prophecies must be encouraging.

I have some stories, amusing now, of how his words have been applied. None of this necessarily reflects upon the brother prophet who originally gave the advice to moderate how you deliver words. Everybody's messages are distorted. I just want to stress that as a prophet, indeed merely giving a gift of any prophetic word, you are a mail carrier. Just deliver the word exactly as you were given it. It is not about you. You are to deliver it accurately. And in order. This is important.

And by the way, prophecies directed at people are much less common than prophecies meant for an assembled congregation! There are prophecies for individuals and for nations, but probably not many, and usually not very often given to newbies. And those given to people are nearly always given to people who more or less asked for them by virtue of being at the altar in the context of worship. You can see how normally in such a case, these are encouraging messages. Yes, one should be very careful about delivering personal messages, especially incorrectly.

Here is an example, so you can see what I mean. From a very young believer blossoming into being a prophet, with great talent, I was given an important message having to do with the conduct of my broadcast ministry. But later she changed it with an addition that meant essentially the opposite. So which was it? In the end, I realized I could not depend upon what I was told, if she was not diligent the get the exact and whole message, nor deliver it correctly.

My apologies for failing to mentor her correctly, although she asked me. At that time I did not appropriately know her, that the prophets who inspired her did not mentor, nor the milieu of the prophetic schools in town. All this learning was part of what inspired this book.

I certainly would not argue with someone teaching prophecy who made a rule for his class that in that class all prophecies for people must be encouraging. Indeed, it might be good advice to speak every message in an encouraging way. Marketers know what they are doing when they say everyone is tuned into WII FM: "what is in it for me." So, great, in evangelizing and in discipling and in general exhortation, if you can be faithful to what the Lord said and say it more encouragingly, more positively fine. I just feel the need to weigh in for balance.

Again, what I would stress to any one embarking on learning the prophetic, is to see yourself as a dutiful mail carrier. If you are in service having a vision, wait until you know the vision is finished. Ask God what it means. Ask God how you should deliver it, if you don't already know. For me, when I was young, the order in the service and house was clear. I did not need to ask. But in other situations, still, I must ask to whom, how, and when to deliver the message. God will let you know.

Further, when giving a prophecy, I work to deliver it word for word, exactly as given. If I am not sure about what the exact words are, I wait before the Lord, until I am sure. Sometimes, however, I am told by others that God insists one speak before one is given the whole message. Just listen and be obedient.

God speaks in a variety of ways. And we listen in a variety of ways. Sometimes God gives word for word messages that are delivered word for word. Sometimes God gives a visual message. When that happens, I wait before the Lord on how to express it. Sometimes God gives impressions. When that happens, I never say "Thus saith the Lord"; instead I say "I have the impression..."

Occasionally I have a bodily feeling or another impression that means something not necessarily to be mentioned. For instance, I was asked to join in prayer for a woman before a church service and I got indications that she was sexually abused so that I could pray better with her. Later she told us that she was a prostitute. Of course, many times in the healing ministry, the minister may feel something that indicates what the physical problem is and where the healing will take place. Of course we see on television people having words of knowledge about healing. However, other things might happen. I have had the experience of smelling some odor that clued me in on the kind of spirit around. I figured that was a kind of discerning of spirits. I have had some wisdom come out of my mouth as an answer to someone and been surprised and impressed – because I had not known that before. I figured that must be a word of wisdom. In all of these, God will also give you wisdom about how to share.

Please let me go back to the situation where I was asked to pray for a woman and I had some bodily sensations. Some details may be instructive. Someone else had counseled her, but asked me to come and pray with them. During that prayer time, I listened and was given the word. I gave the verbal and picture word exactly as I could. I was not so sure about sharing the bodily feeling I had. I suspected it meant that she had been raped, so I was going to be very careful how I brought it up, if at all. Turned out that this woman had come in off the street to go to service, had been living a very rough life.

The other woman, like me waiting for service, had engaged her in conversation and had ended up counseled her. It turned out that the counseling woman was an evangelist. I was not in on that conversation, but it included the prayed for woman rededicating herself to the Lord and discussions of steps to get off the street. I was given the impression of a pink and yellow very soft baby blanket. I talked about how the Holy Spirit is a comforter, and of course more than a blanket, but that this picture could be used, and specifically how troubling thoughts come, but that she could "wrap the baby blanket around her head" and speak the Name of Jesus. How this was useful in times of fear, in times of being cold, and in times of troubled thoughts. Maybe this application was a word of wisdom? Surely I was continuing to ask God how to express the vision and continuing to listen. The feeling in my body I interpreted to mean that she had been raped. Later she did tell us that she had been involved with prostitution and clearly was troubled.

The point of the story is not to tell you her story or even my experience, but to give an idea of how to handle the messages.. In this case, besides the words and pictures, there may be sensation. That was not something to blurt out immediately. There was a clear sense, however, of what to say when I later found out her plight. Her response made it clear that it had been correct and helpful. I might have mentioned the feeling or asked about the experience had I been the counselor. As it was, however, it simply clued me into the seriousness and direction of the advice.

So I agree that we must watch how we deliver, but while the other brother may stress being encouraging, I want to also stress being as exact as possible. If I have an impression or a feeling, I would use that language. If I have a leading or a "feeling," I say so. If I say "Thus saith the Lord" then I have the message exact, word for word and I should hope even correct intonation. If I have a picture, I attempt to convey it correctly. I often wait for clear instruction and often default to my original instructions of how to write it down and turn it in to the one presiding. It's about being a good communicator and everything we do communicates.

7 **My Advice**

How I Was Trained

Actually I was not "trained." There were clear rules in the movement I was a part of when I was young. I had just moved, newly in a local body. At breakfast, the elders asked if I were a prophet. Clearly they hoped so. So when I was praying that morning, I told God I was open to being the carrier of any gift He had for His Body. I had my first vision. Looking back, it was a challenging vision, inasmuch as it was so simple, and so in context that one might have doubted. But I knew I had seen a vision. So I gave it. I continued to have visions both in service and when requested by the elders' meeting. When I left that congregation, the leading elder told me that my visions were very clear. This was something that was never done in that movement as far as I knew, so I counted it a huge encouragement.

Now, we are not told to just be open, we are told to seek very heartily after the gifts, but I remain open to the gifts that God would give His body. I meant whatever one, whichever ones. I will tell you of the experiences I had and the order in that group. This is not to tell you that this order should be the correct one. Indeed, I will tell you to work with the elders, the pastor, where you are. Many of the rules are meaningful only for that particular situation, and some may be arbitrary or even wrong. So what? This is part of "the spirits of the prophets are subject to the prophets" I Co 14: 32 or [the prophecy is under the speaker's control, and he can stop speaking]; *Amplified.*

In the movement where I was as a young person, visions were very highly regarded. Prophecy or tongues and interpretation may be given during the song service before the preaching, or possibly afterward, but there was a precise order desired about visions. Visions were especially highly regarded because of the desire to be cutting edge revelation and because of the thought that prophets confirmed the word of the apostle, visions were thought to be less liable to manipulation and thus highly reliable and desirable. So during the song service I would see a vision, write it down, and it would be read after the preaching, during the closing of the service. It was hoped that the vision would confirm the word preached. Amazingly, it always did. (Well, it did back in those years. In more recent years many of us received dis-confirmatory visions. This proved to be unpleasant, but the fact that all the prophets had the same experience told us something.) We were to write it down in block letters, and sign and date it. The signing and dating illustrated how important these were. We were staking our reputation on this.

I am not suggesting that anyone go out and try to be cutting edge, or depend upon visions to confirm what they are preaching. Rather, I would very much urge that all preaching be not only prophetic but also clearly based on clear exegesis of Scripture. Getting away from Scripture is no doubt the cause of those dis-confirmatory visions. However, that God speaks the same thing to the preachers and to the prophets, and did for years was very instructive.

By the way, in this group, there were often more than one preacher during any given service. In those years it was expected that the preachers would all preach on the same subject, without first conferring with one another. When I was 16, I participated in this. (Btw, I am not sure they knew I was only 16, but the majority of the congregation was under 20.) I would kneel by my bed, ask

God what to study. I would be given a Scripture to read, then be given a word to preach from it and at least 2 more passages. I always preached first. Messages always matched – for 6 months, twice a week. To be clear: all the other preachers preached on the same topic, without any conference ahead of time with me. I preached first, so I had no natural cues. The Spirit flowed with one voice for the 6 months I was preaching, twice a week, until I was transferred to a different location. Back in those days, the quarterly conventions were similar: traveling ministers and head elders from local congregations would be able to sit on the platform and preach, as they felt lead. We had maybe 20-50 people sitting on the platform and maybe as many as 3,000 in the hall. We had a week of two services a day, each lasting at least 4 hours. There was no schedule nor previously published topic. Any time two people stood up to go to the lectern, it was assumed that at least one had missed the Lord. It seldom happened. A theme usually emerged. That was a high bar. It doesn't happen anymore, but it was a good school for me.

Even in recent years, participating in regular congregations, I found that often my prophecy in the pre-service intercessory prayer time or song service matched the pastor's sermon topic. For sure he had prepared ahead and for sure I had no way of knowing what the topic was. So the pattern holds. Indeed, I look for this pattern to be sure it is Holy Spirit leading everyone.

Prophets were used confirm leadings. A person with an important leading, such as moving to another body/congregation to another, he or she would meet with the elders (i.e. plural clergy, like a committee of local pastors). The elders would then phone prophets of choice and ask for visions. I would be told, "We need 4 visions, one for each of 3 men and one for a woman." That is all I would be told. I would not be told something such as 2 of these men are moving, one is looking for work and the woman wonders if she should divorce her husband. No, I was told nothing. I would get the number of visions and deliver them in writing to the elders and not hear anything more about it. This was the pattern throughout the Move. Prophets were expected not to be curious about the mail they delivered.

For instance, once I saw a vision for a man that included a man (though I did not see who) get in a car, that wouldn't go, and the ignition didn't work, and the car was in a mud puddle. So apparently I guess this guy wasn't flowing in the Spirit and had some issue with carnality? At the time I didn't ask or expect any interpretation because in that group only elders interpreted. Of course, I don't know the situation even today, but you see how the imagery is readable.

The elders would deliver the visions and interpret them, just as they would interpret visions at the end of service. If the meaning was not clear from Scripturally encultured meaning, they would ask the Lord for understanding.

Prophets were also used during casting out demons. Elders might want to be informed about the progress, direction, or kind of situation they with which they were dealing. Further, anytime people were being prayed for by the congregation or the eldership, words of prophesy or visions (which is the same thing in visual rather than verbal form) might be given. For instance, if some where were "set in" (i.e. ordained) or going to a new location the group might gather round and be given words, by anyone, but only under the supervision of the elders. Prophets known in the house might just speak out their visions, but those giving visions in a place where they are not known and trusted, would write down the vision and hand it to an elder, who would then read it and hand it on to the person assuming they didn't think it was inappropriate. Personally, I have never had an elder not pass on one of my visions. I have read on social media of a young person making up a vision and getting a warm response from the recipient!

It was in this milieu, when I left Oshawa for Headwaters Ranch, that the leading elder told me my visions were clear. Since it was the expectation that I would never know anything, I found this very comforting and instructive.

Today I know people who appear to be prophets and teach others how to prophesy who have never been given any indication whether their prophecies have been "right on" or "a little off." One dear, pitiful woman, who I have seen give false prophecies and who has often been in the worst practices in this city said to me recently, "Well, no one has ever complained." Well you can see how people may be reluctant to complain! People are reluctant.

Sometimes people complain improperly. I think of an international level prophet, well thought of my peers, who has given warnings that haven't come to pass. He says the warnings were heeded, but you can imagine what skeptics say. As much persecution as speaking truth from the pulpit or elsewhere receives, I can imagine that a prophesier might also get similar blowback. I think you can see how all this might conducive to dis-order. Prophetic mentors maybe should give some guidance before setting someone up as a prophet let alone teacher/mentor of prophets.

I have had mature ministers say of platform level prophets "well, I'm sure he meant well." However, the extent to which we do hear strangers "read others' mail" and demonized people walk away sane, one can not discount the power of real prophetic words.

In the group in which I was formed as a prophet, any prophet that was "off" was sat down. Visions that didn't confirm the preached word were not read. This happened seldom in a local congregation: everyone could see how many visions were passed up. In a convention, by contrast, the apostles could decide not to share a vision, and so make them all appear confirmatory. Possibly some notes of other kinds were being passed up to the platform, such as prayer requests or notes about dinner timing. You have to ask someone else, as I was not privy to what was going on up on the platform. I do know that more recently, given the reception of dis-confirmanatory visions, some prophets have stopped delivering words. Others are disrespectful and hap-hazard. Others have not stopped but have been blamed. Of course many have left the movement. I have known of prophets receive judgment/condemnation for dis-confirmatory visions, by apostles who were by then preaching off the wall stuff. Imagine, in a movement that taught *ad nauseum* on the five-fold ministry being like a hand, having a vivid dream of a disconnected thumb! That is a little scary! Would you turn that vision in? I hope you can read the imagery and steel yourself for obedience. Once again, I don't put forth this group as the measure of all things, but only as one instructive example. It is what I can contribute.

Sister Wanda Rankin's (nee James) Perspective

Sister Wanda was an elder and highly regarded prophet from this same movement. She was mature, perhaps in her 40s when I was just a teen, so her experience was even more responsible. She is someone I respect and I feel has been tested over decades in many circumstance. She says that she felt her best duty was to sit in the back and pray over everyone, especially as they came in, and especially anyone new coming in. She might be given some impression or word. Perhaps she might have an impression about someone and therefore go over and speak to them and perhaps offer an encouraging word as a friendly older person. Perhaps she would know to mention to the elders that someone needed prayer or counsel. Only rarely would she prophesy to them in these sorts of instances. Certainly most of her life, she also participated in seeing visions in services or at request of the eldership. She might even still give personal words on request, although she sees very few people these days because of advanced age. The most important point is that this woman, whom I judge to be the most powerful prophet I know, says her best ministry was praying over people as they came into service and the result was rarely some show of prophetic word.

My Current Best Advice on Flowing in Various Congregation

Work with house rules. Understand that various pastors will have various rules. Some will permit you to line up at a microphone. Others will expect you to come and stand beside them to confer, and get permission, before speaking to the congregation. Some will expect you to know how to fit into the flow of the song service, and fit in as appropriate. You will not interrupt. If it is a

Spirit led service, and the Spirit gives you a word, there will be a lull for you. If it is not a Spirit led service, there will probably not be an opening for a gift; you would be seen as disrupting, and this we don't do. Well, some senior Old Testament prophet might, but I certainly don't advise you to, and I wouldn't unless I was sure, very very very sure God definitely told me to. And even then I probably wouldn't -- God help me.

Not knowing house rules, I often revert to writing it down and passing up to the pastor's chair. In most congregations where I get visions, the pastor and his wife sit on the first row, so passing up to his chair makes sense. Occasionally I have had to just mention something to the pastor at the end of service.

Often, given the ubiquity of sound equipment, the use of gifts is relegated to prayer meetings these days. I know at least one Pentecostal preacher laments the dearth of gifts because of the broadcasting necessities. So he invited it more into altar time and intercessory prayer time before service.

It is not generally appropriate to be giving private personal words. Do not pull someone into the copier room. Do not permit accosting people in the bathroom. If personal words are not given where pastor and other prophets can judge, it is not given in order nor Biblically. Do not do this and do not permit it.

Now, you may, like a friend, speak a word and say to your friend, "I kinda feel like..." But do not be claiming to be a prophet and be doing private personal words. Surely don't take them. You don't want a word from a prophet out of order. Remember, there are false prophets.

If it is really necessary to convey something to someone not in public or at a distance, then write it down and send it. That way they can show it to others. This method is particular useful if you have something for your pastor. Giving him direction in front of the congregation is normally not appropriate. Of course, friends all of whom are prophetic and are used to leading together will give themselves leeway, but my advice is for default guidance.

Being out and evangelizing is another story. Some people "go shopping" for salvations elicited by healings or spiritual manifestations. Other people go on a "treasure hunt." How can we be against that? It is like Peter and John at the Gate Beautiful. I would suggest going out two-by-two. I have even seen a prayer tent at a Christmas Bethlehem Village and heard of a booth at a wild fair that was styled like a fortune teller booth. Fine. I would just urge wisdom. Maybe get a mentor of a mature minister or prophet. But, by all means, evangelize and listen to God and be obedient! Good job!

My Current Advice to Pastors

Pastors often do not realize how they powerfully they play in the wider picture. When we have a paucity of the prophetic often it is because pastors prevent it. When we do have the prophetic show up in an unhealthy way it is often because of what pastors have and have not done. It might be good news to some pastors that there are some things they can do to both spread the prophetic and ensure good order.

Pastors are often scared spitless about what prophets will do. Well, pastors, you should know that pentecostal pastors have long discussed how to handle prophets and intercessors, etc. Here is my advice. You want the gifts. You want the Word of God to flow fully. You will be blessed to have some prophets around. A prophet is God's gift to you, so says Ephesians 4:11. At the same time, you do not want false prophets and if you permit them, you are Ahab. There are never Jezebels unless there are Ahabs. Ahab brought in Jezebel and profited from her. Similarly, Absolom's father failed out of indulgence and unwise love. He didn't reign in some of his sons. Similarly, pastors make space for disorder when they don't take up leadership properly themselves, and they tempt people who have leadership capacity by failing to deploy them well.

So be sure you are in touch with God yourself, Then make some rules; make a format. Teach on the gifts. Listen to the Spirit yourself. Create an expectation that the Spirit will flow with the Spirit. Teach your people well enough that they can spot a false spirit, creating strife or arrogance or carnality a mile off.

There is no such office as Intercessor except Jesus' own ministry! It is just not in the Bible. The reason it is important to say this is because sometimes intercessors attempt to control the pastor or the house with their gift. This is inappropriate. Of course, at the same time, we should appreciate gifted people and provide legitimate leadership opportunities. Not doing so is an invitation to disorder. There are some people who really are good, even gifted, intercessors, but we are all supposed to intercede. Some of these "intercessors" may be called to be prophets. Many are simply gifted pray-ers. Pastors, do not let them lead meetings unless you are certain they understand how to be under authority and you teach them how to be in authority. I have seen a pastor go so far as to specify in writing what was to be prayed for in the meeting. They prayed for him, but only in precisely prescribed words. People still came to prayer meeting. Teach your whole congregation about authority, and then when someone tries to build a barony for themselves, it won't just be you who sees it. By contrast, if you continue to be scared of this eventuality and insist on being the only one who runs meetings, you will ensure you have a small church. Just do not let an "intercessor" attempt to control you. Real prophets will self effacingly submit words and not try to control you. When I hear a word from God, it doesn't make me proud and controlling; it makes me a certain kind of serious, reverent and in awe. The feeling is really opposite of imposing and controlling.

Some, including Bobby Conner. suggest that witches infiltrate intercessor circles. I certainly have seen them attempt to "contribute" to meetings. This also maybe true of false prophets. I assume every circle has some newbies who may not quite have it all right. So fine, just as every congregation has an authority system and a way to organize services and in group and personal life, lovingly correct and get things back on track, so should every prayer group. Bobby Conner suggests that every prayer meeting begin with "Hallowed be Thy Name" because witches have a hard time praying that. Others always pray the blood of Jesus and specifically pray against demons. I do not believe there is one certain formula. I have heard of a demon spouting "I plead the blood!" fast and furiously as resistance to being cast out! I do think, however, in a healthily lead group, there will be numerous times to speak by the Spirit, to witness what is going on, and numerous ways to "take authority." What is most important is for the pastor to instruct, empower, and stand behind a trustworthy person doing so. It is very difficult for a pastor, let alone lay person, to stand up to many who might bring disorder because of their popularity or standing within the community. So I hope these suggestions empower pastors to organize the situation so as to avoid problems.

I think right here is the rub. Many who would seek attention will venture into the spiritual, make really bad trouble before either being reigned in or things explode. Pastors know that to stopping problems elicits political difficulties, so demonic problems seem to grow covertly. Pastors are going around in their flesh, too busy to pray, because they are overworked, and rightfully scared of demons attacking them and crazies trying to control them. Then intercessors and prophets, are going around frustrated that they have no outlet and no teaching. So in immaturity they do something a bit wrong. Or maybe rightly but in a slightly offensive. Then they are shut down. And move to another church. And the pastor is happy. Oh dear. Then for years everyone wonders why things are so dry.

We should have healthy ministerial order in order to grow into full maturity of Christlikeness as a body. We should go from Ephesians 4:11 to grow into Ephesians 4:12-16. You are praying for the wind of the Spirit, and teaching toward maturity, and hoping for a church growing in the image of Christ, yes? Following the books on the latest seeker-sensitive fad will not get it, only Truth of Bible and Spirit.

- Everyone defers to the other
- All hear from the Lord
- Each does his/her part

O by the way, if you were more Biblical, and let leading women lead in proper fashion, you might not have bad stuff squishing out so much. Leading women will head off the bad ones. And maybe fewer bad ones would develop. So often, though, good leaders are quashed, and bad leaders in charge, who then don't see disastrous people coming. Furthermore, people who might have developed into strong leaders are twisted into manipulative covert operatives precisely because they have been taught not to lead. The whole body suffers.

8 Situations About Which I Am Concerned

1. Prophecies that are not from God.

Maybe I could just stop there, because this just about covers it.

My personal unfavorite is when upon getting a prophecy and not showing that I am particularly impressed, then I get the opposite prophecy. This indicates to me that the person is willing to "prophesy" anything in order to get status. Trouble is, that I have been in this experience multiple times. Since this is unlikely to happen to a pastor known to the person prophesying, I think it would be a fine idea to send in a friend to take a reading of the health of the prophesying, whether in your intercessors group, altar workers, women's group or whatever.

I understand the desire to mentor more into the prophetic, but I worry that a pecuniary interest has blinded people into getting others okay with just saying stuff, as if it were prophecy. Sometimes it is just young persons being ignorant. Sometimes it is a few who want to push themselves forward as if they were leaders. Sometimes it is a situation of unbalanced teaching: seeking the gifts without also seeking character; attempting to get to glorification without sanctification.

A concern with "schools of the prophets" type training is that the exercises "throw people in the water to begin to swim" possibly encouraging meeting people's expectations rather than practice listening to God. If the leadership and the examples are engaging in aggrandizement and fake practices, then this will even more encourage fake prophecy!

I am concerned about a great deal of "training" maybe because I have never seen anyone who is a prophet who was ever trained to be one, and I certainly never was trained. Instead I was given strict protocol. It was up to God to give me prophecy and up to me to listen. However, okay, since we are commanded to seek the prophetic and since there were schools of the prophets during the Old Testament days, maybe it is okay – even good for the times. There is a place for practical education. The result simply depends upon the people involved.

Further, I am concerned that after 10 years of several prophetic schools in my metro area, there is no increase in number of salvations, church attendance, or reputation of the prophetic. I have seen only sad results. I do hope that my sample is not representative, but it is a definite enough observation to merit discussion. I do pray for some good fruit showing up soon, and I think God for many brothers and sisters working in this area.

2. Prophets out to garner attention through being flashy, obvious, or weird

Of course, I could tell you more stories about people acting weird and drawing attention to themselves through the use of gifts. By contrast, gifts from God focus on helping the recipient and bring glory to God. The most powerful prophet I personally know has already told us what she thinks her greatest contribution is, and notice, that it would seem very unobvious to most people. I think most great people are like that. Some may have a calling to be outgoing and need to be flashy, but it is all about God. Maybe we can even overlook a certain amount of pride in leadership, but we don't therefore think that it is spiritual.

I see people prophesying but failing to "unfold" the Word of God – meaning they so focus on their prophesying that they don't preach or teach. That might be fine on occasion, but I am concerned about a congregation who builds itself in this manner, likely failing to properly build the character of its congregants.

I could tell you stories of silly behavior concocted to make a show and gain status. I remember a woman making a show right after service closing. I can take you to a regional woman's meeting where people vy to be seen as prophets. Alas, I can tell you of pastors who forgot they were at pastors meetings, so busy they were at showing off. Given what Ezekiel did, I wouldn't pass judgment on the weird -- unless it was aimed at claiming superior status and was proven wrong. Young people seem particularly susceptible to the leadership of pride clothed in spookiness.

In one congregation here, with some sort of prophetic school, there is a small coterie of lay people who are encouraged to do "spiritual" stuff out of order. For instance, in an event where a guest speaker came to talk and several churches came together to hear him, one of these people was throwing people down to the point that the guest speaker told him to stop. I was encouraged to stand in line for an out of town guest speaker to pray for me. Instead, this little band of three grabbed me and started prophesying. Notice, they had no permission from me to do so. I'm not sure they had permission from whoever was in charge of the meeting, either. The first prophesied that I would be given a ministry to 9 year olds because for 9 years I had fought the Pro-life fight so faithfully. Well, I had been ordained many years and had never fought any pro-life fight. Then the second man grabbed my hand and prophesied release from my legalistic background. Since I have had a similar prophecy before, (see below) I was not completely caught unawares. I took him by the hand and asked if he meant my UPC background. He said yes, indicating that he understood that I understood. Except that I have no UPC background! I did not feel I needed any release from any legalistic background. I was reared in a liberal Methodist home and was at that time an instructor of Sociology! Then I turned to someone who is supposed to have earned a doctorate. I was hoping that since I was pinned in by these three, at least I would get something less crazy from him. But alas, no words. He in the habit of just grabbing an arm and throwing people to the floor. Well, I didn't want to be thrown, so leaned against the wall. I just had to wait for them to leave. Great prophets – not. They think they are leaders in this town. Worse, maybe they are.

3. People "prophesying" from their own prejudices, rather than words from God.

We should not be "prophesying" through "seeing of the eye," meaning what everyone can see. There was a congregation here supposedly associated with a longtime, well known prophet. I have visited several times but never heard a sermon. Once a guest speaker interrupted himself to prophesy out to me that I would be released from my legalistc background. Hmmm. I took it seriously at first. Later, I realized that I was wearing a long skirt and had my hair up. I guess I didn't have enough make up on to have it seen from the platform. LOL Seeing my mode of dress, he gave a prophecy aimed at tearing me away from my legalistic background -- which never existed. Well, you see what I mean about false prophecies.

I have non-Christian friends who are into yoga and the occult who similarly think they can read minds. For instance, I handed my hammer to one of these friends, because he was going to fix my front door. He started talking about my feelings of lack of trust toward him. Oh, how spiritual he was to read minds. I explained to him I only owned a small hammer because I have small, woman sized hands. He was appropriately embarrassed.

On the other hand, since I mentioned my spiritual but non-Christian friend, please let me throw in here, that it must be admitted that some of these people are successful with supernatural experience. Some of the group that my carpenter friend belongs to do get into others' dreams, unbidden, to recruit them. One of my purportedly Buddhist friends is such a good meditator that he found himself inside a woman friend's body, seeing from her eyes. He decided maybe he should quit; that such violated her privacy. So that is a concern also, supernatural experience from the Adamic nature, or may it not be so, the evil spirits.

4. People adopting the form while denying there could be anything supernatural about "speaking forth"

I know a particular church where people do the motions of prophecy, meaning people come up and say stuff to members just like in churches were people believe in prophecy, but this church does not believe in the Baptism of the Holy Spirit. So while some charismatic people seeing this behavior are joining what they think is a charismatic and prophetic church, it really is not. Similarly, their worship service is planned to look like a Spirit-led service, but it is not. I would urge reading the church's doctrinal statement. This church indicates fairly clearly that they are against manifestations of Holy Spirit. They are just doing outwardly what is popular.

Similarly, some have misconstrued the "be encouraging" word. I knew well a woman who claimed to be in the inner circle of a well known stage prophet who perhaps taught that all prophecies must be encouraging. Somehow she changed this advice in her mind to : when "a friend" needs encouragement, "prophesy" to her. So she makes up spiritual sounding stuff. In this manner, she grooms a following. Similarly, I have had the experience of someone, not at all claiming to be a prophet, (indeed who is fairly mixed up and likely mentally ill, possibly even demonized), who upon hearing this other gal "prophesying" wrote out a similar verse on a card and handed it to me. Only later did I discover that she had heard what the first woman had said. Only later did I get to know her. She said she had just wanted to participate. Bless her heart. Good thing I didn't take any advice from such a situation that contradicted sense or my own hearing!

There is also a possibility of demons lying and giving prophecies, so people are really into spiritual experience, but not speaking the Word of God. If there are not other prophets judging, because it is private or hidden experience, then there is a great danger. There have been some instances of dangerous people creating apparent relationships, calling on the phone to prophesy, and eventually prophesying a bunch of money transferred to themselves!!!

6.   Using prophecy as a way to even a score against someone who you don't like, didn't like your sermon, or whatever.

Enough said. Well, no. People do get away with this. "You pass on a word from God?" they say. But using the Lord's Name in vain is very serious. Evening the score in the here and now, might end up with God's wrath in the hereafter.

Using spiritual gifts, even real, in attempt to coerce and control people is quite similar. Very scary.

7.   Using prophecy as self aggrandizement. By the way, it doesn't work.

One pastor in our town, at a meeting for pastors, sat at the table and without leave or appropriate context, just starting prophesying over everyone to show off. He prophesied over me that I would be taking over the protesting at the abortion clinic in my neighborhood. Well, there isn't one. I wouldn't have been interested. And he really was surprised that I was not interested and wouldn't even pray about it. What is there to pray about? Well, maybe for him. Incidentally, he doesn't have a congregation anymore. Same story with all levels of trying to show off. People eventually notice.

By contrast, to the more timid, please let me encourage you. People are following flawed leadership because that is the best they see. Do not be afraid to move out in obedience. Come good or ill. We need you. Even will ill comes, keep going. We need you.

So, in summary:

No more denying the prophetic.

No more private prophecies at church.

No more using the prophetic to merely show off – or worse.

No more using the nonexistent office of the Intercessor or prophet to subvert pastoral direction.

No more Pastors suppressing the development of spiritual gifts because of fear of Jezebels, etc.

No more disrespecting prophets who didn't go through your particular school.

No more failing to make protocol known.

9 Don't Be Afraid; It Is All About Jesus

Listen to God. It is acceptable to ask to be sure you heard. Deliver as accurately as possible. Don't be disrespectful of the church or its leadership while doing so. Seek to do this and keep your flesh out of the way. By the way, it is real very fun.

Okay, so some advice in general: try to communicate correctly about how sure you are. Do you sort of feel like God is saying …? Do you have a leading? Do you have an impression? Do you have a picture in your mind? Or what is definitely a supernatural vision? (For me visions are not like me imagining a purple elephant. A vision is an experience that I am not able to reproduce.) And open vision (meaning you saw it with the eyes of your body.) Is this your understanding that you think you have been given just now? Do you have a Word from the Lord, word for word as in "thus saith the Lord"? It is not always necessary to advertise that you have been given what you are saying. Sometimes it really doesn't help. Most of the time, being specific does help. I would suggest being as clear as is useful without overstepping. You can have difficulty by overclaiming and by under delivering, both. Aim at accuracy.

Don't get overly involved with who is a prophet and who is not or what level of a prophet they are. Who cares? Well, people who want to make a name for themselves as being a prophet might have some investment in being sure someone else is not considered one. Look, in a congregation, it becomes clear who is trusted. Surely they are prophets (see I Cor 14) even if they are not predicting the national future from stages. I know a missionary who made a drought stop, but he doesn't claim to be a prophet. He doesn't seem to care about a new title. The region turned to God. Even with traveling stage level prophets, what is really important is the connection with the Lord they encourage. Was Jonah a real prophet? His prophecies didn't come true. We know of only his experience in Nineveh and not any school or prophetic career in Israel. Who cares? The Ninevites came to the Lord and that was the point.

Please don't be afraid! These concerns are in order to make a confusing situation more clear. Rules are guidelines to make people feel safe and know how to proceed. Pastors have a very very very difficult task. Fear of the prophetic should be marked off the list, once they have some ideas about what to do and some practice in implementing such measures. Most of all, people should listen to God and share what they are hearing. Gosh, so what if you got it a tad wrong? Isn't that what a healthy congregation should do for you? Be a good group to run with, so you are encouraged and kept on track? Even prophets, please go forward, now with less fear.

Oh, false ones, have the fear of God! Be turned toward His mercy and great reality. Let as all repent of any falseness! Oh, teachers, I know you have the fear of God. We are judged more harshly. Gosh. Well. Let's consecrate ourselves to do His best, yes? When we are corrected about pride, let's reverse course. When we learn something new, let's incorporate that new, better way. Really, in our teaching, we have to contribute. We must. Failing to teach isn't very good either. So as Luther said, whatever we do, let's do it with our whole selves, and unafraid.

What makes good prophecy? Let's us argue from definitions? God is the only good one. God is both orderly and wild. LOL!

I have long wondered about the words in Revelation that the testimony of Jesus is the spirit of prophecy (Rev 19:10). Hmm, as I write this I think this is the mark of good prophecy: it brings you closer to Jesus. Hope you have arrived at that same point with me. Keep your eyes upon Jesus!

Then, when I look more at that verse, I deduce that the angels are particularly here to serve those to who testify to Jesus prophetically. I will also hazard the opinion that learning a prophetic lifestyle is an important step in growing up into being like Jesus (Ro 8:14). So let's not draw back, but rather proceed; but proceed with due reverence, great reverence, even awe.

So let's thank the Lord for the precious gifts He has given us, both the manifestation of Holy Spirit that we call the gifts and also the ones we call ministries. Let's envision, pray for, and prophesy into being a robust congregations and strong wider church community, mighty with supernatural guidance, encouragement and demonstration. I am not just writing this to have a nice flourish with which to finish. Rather, I am suggesting this is how we proceed. I just heard Lance Wallnau say not only does what you focus attract; but also what you energize, activates. So he began praying thanking God for what he wanted. So let's pray into more prophetic and better order with thanksgiving and praise. Lord, help us see You and represent You! Come, Holy Spirit within us! Grow us! Make us ready for Jesus Messiah coming back!

ABOUT THE AUTHOR

Sharon began serving as a prophet in 1976 in an Apostolic & Prophetic Movement that grew out of the Latter Rain. She has served in pastoral leadership in three very different denominations. She has retired from college teaching but continues to write, broadcast, train and consult. She lives in Austin, Texas.

www.greatshalom.org
www.thegovernmentisnotavillage.com
www.orgstrat.net

www.ingramcontent.com/pod-product-compliance
Lightning Source LLC
Chambersburg PA
CBHW060709030426
42337CB00017B/2811